Chameleon's Clever

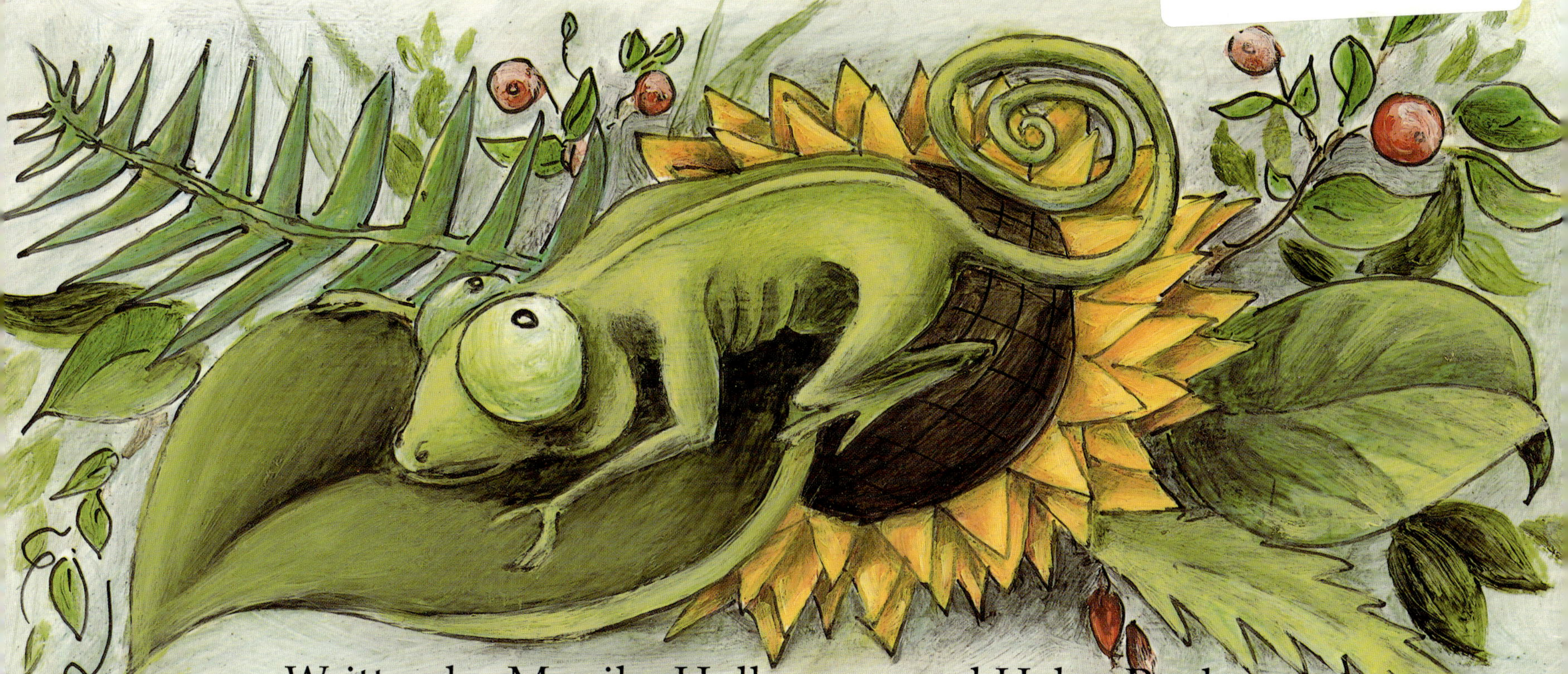

Written by Monika Hollemann and Helen Pooler
Workshopped with Ntombizine Kom
and Madoda Matiwane

Illustrated by Monika Hollemann

Chameleon crawled carefully along a bush. Her eyes rolled forwards, upwards, downwards, backwards.

"Ooh! Look at that big, fat, juicy fly!
I hope I can catch it," she said.

Chameleon ignored Mouse.
She gripped the branch with her tail.
Then she shot out her long, sticky tongue
and flicked the fly into her mouth.

"Yum," said Chameleon turning pink with pleasure.
"Do you still think I'm slow?" she asked Mouse.

"Well, maybe your tongue is fast.
But *you* can't run away from a cat
like I can," replied Mouse.

"I don't have to run. I can make myself invisible. Just watch me!" said Chameleon.

Chameleon climbed onto a dark, purple leaf. Magically her skin started to change to purple – exactly the same colour as the leaf!

"Hey! Where have you gone?" squeaked Mouse.
He looked up, down and all around. Then he saw her on the leaf.
"Huh? How did you do that?"

"Aha!" said Chameleon proudly. "That's my special trick."
"Well," said Mouse, "I bet you can't change to yellow."

Chameleon moved across
to a yellow sunflower.
Mouse looked and looked.
Little by little,
Chameleon turned as yellow as a sunflower.

Then clever Chameleon stepped on to the warm brick wall and turned red... with stripes! "Mouse! Can you see me now?"
Mouse didn't like being tricked but Chameleon was enjoying herself. As they argued, a shadow crept quietly nearer.

"Maybe you can change your colour but you've got a silly, curly tail and funny, rolling eyes!" Mouse carried on squeaking.

"Yes! But hanging by my curly tail and using my rolling eyes, I can see Cat behind you! *Look out!*" shouted Chameleon.

"**Meeeoouw!**" Cat pounced on Mouse.
"**Eeek!**" squeaked Mouse.

"What can I do?" thought Chameleon. Quickly, she used another clever trick. She turned dangerously dark and hissed loudly. **"Kkkkkkhhhhh!"**

Cat got such a fright, he dropped Mouse, and ran away.

"Thank you, Chameleon." gasped Mouse.
"You saved me with your clever trick.
But Chameleon... where are you?"
Somewhere on a green bush
Mouse heard Chameleon laughing.
She was up to her tricks again!
Mouse couldn't see her at all!
Can *you*?